# Faithful Finances Forever

## A Guide to Being Faithful in Your Finances

by Keith Wilson

*I know what it is to be in need, and I know what it is to have plenty.
I have learned the secret of being content in any and every situation, whether
well fed or hungry, whether living in plenty or in want. I can do all this through
Him who gives me strength.*

*Philippians 4:12-13*

# Dedication

*First and foremost, this book is dedicated to my Lord and Savior Jesus Christ.*

*I would not have been able to write this book if it were not for His grace*

*and mercy.*

# Table of Contents

# 1. Introduction

*Those who accepted His message were baptized and about three thousand were added to their number that day. They devoted themselves to the apostles teaching and to the fellowship; to the breaking of bread and to prayer. Everyone was filled with awe and many wonders and miraculous signs were done by the apostles. All the believers were together and had everything in common. Selling their possessions and goods, they gave to anyone as he had need. Every day they continued to meet together in the temple courts. They broke bread in their homes and ate together with glad and sincere hearts, praising God and enjoying the favor of all the people and the Lord added to their numbers daily those who were being saved.*

*Acts 2:41-47 (NIV)*

When I first read the above verse I began to wonder would I ever see this type of society. In the above text we see a community that had all things in common and they shared with one another. The individualistic mindset of today's society causes us to only focus on ourselves and not on how God wants us to be in managing our finances. So when it comes to our own finances, we are doing things our own way and not allowing God to direct us. When we allow God to direct our finances we will attain Faithful Finances Forever.

One day I was driving down 56th Street here in Indianapolis and I came to a red light. While waiting at the light a car pulled up beside me. It was a very nice vehicle with a man inside that looked very distinguished. We eventually looked at each other and gave the nod. Based on the vehicle, it appeared that he was successful and well off. I proceeded to roll down my window to ask him if he had any words of wisdom that he could share about his success, but the light turned green and he took off. While he was driving off, I noticed his license plate said, "Got Mine." I drove away from that encounter thinking, "If he got his how I can get mine?" This moment made me realize there was another gospel that people are living by and it's called the gospel according to Madison Avenue. A gospel, that even I as a Christian, began following which eventually led to my financial destruction.

# My Story

I was born and raised in Queens, New York. My mom and dad knew of God, but they did not have a relationship with God. My dad was the breadwinner and my mom stayed home to take care of the family. We lived off of one income and did not have money to do a lot of things including taking vacations. I graduated from St. John's University with a Bachelor's degree in Finance and with a goal to get a high paying job upon graduation. I was told that with a Finance degree in New York, my salary should be in the range of 20k-25k per year. It was to my disappointment that when I graduated, the only company that would hire me paid me 11k per year. I spent the next 25 years seeking higher incomes because I was never content with what I was being paid. This is a problem we've taught the next generation. We tell them they need to make a lot of money, but we have not taught them how to be content with what they have.

My income increased over time, but I was spending more than I was making. As a single man living at home, I did not have to pay rent. My company gave me a car, so I did not have to purchase one. I bought my first home at 25 years old and was not ready for the expenses that came with it. Ironically, my parents bought their first home when they were in their early 50's.

I got married at 26 and went further into debt. I relocated with the company several times, had two children, and eventually ended up in Indiana. We continued spending more than we earned and bought a five-bedroom 4500 square foot home that was over our head. We could not save any money, tithe, or go on vacation. My ex-wife and I had different views on money and because we were not equally yoked in the area of money management we ended up getting a divorce after 20 years of marriage. The divorce devastated me financially. I had to get a three-bedroom apartment so when the children came over they would have their own room. The first two years after the divorce was hard and I could not make ends meet. I had to reach out to my church's food pantry to get food. I had no furniture or television. I started going to Goodwill for household things like pots, pans, cups, and glassware. Even though I did not have much, my children were just happy to be with me.

I gradually began to get back on my feet and eventually re-married. My current wife and I are equally yoked especially when it comes to our finances. We watch our spending, spend less than we earn, pay our tithes, and save. What I am about to share with you in the coming pages helped me understand that my worldly mindset had to be changed to a biblical mindset in order to produce fruit that was pleasing to God. This changed mindset helped me to achieve a life of Faithful Finances Forever.

# 2. The Gospel According to Madison Avenue

The gospel according to Madison Avenue is an individualistic mindset in which we labor for ourselves and not for others. Over the years, we have moved from working and sharing with those in the community to an individualistic mindset that says the following:

*"Got Mine"*

*"Get all you can, can all you get"*

*"You must keep up with the Jones'"*

*"The person with the most toys wins"*

*"I owe, I owe so off to work I go"*

There was a time when the master worked side by side with his apprentice. In many cases, the apprentice lived with the master subject to the same conditions of the master. When the apprentice rose to the master's level, he or she would educate and train the next apprentice in the same way they were trained. This brought about equality, not individualism. Today, I see a society that is not looking to give a hand up. We are so focused on ourselves that we forget about our neighbor. Growing up, I was never told about the proper way of handling money, but I had the head knowledge because of my Bachelor's Degree in Finance and a MBA in Financial Planning. Even with these degrees, I still managed money my way. It was not until I gave my life to Christ that I realized there was a different way to manage money. After living a certain way for many years, it was hard to follow God's way of managing money. I am reminded of the lyrics of the Frank Sinatra song "My Way" which says,

*"And now, the end is near*

*And so I face the final curtain*

*My friend, I'll say it clear*

*I'll state my case, of which I'm certain*

*I've lived a life that's full*

*I've traveled each and every highway*

*But more, much more than this*

*I did it my way*

*Regrets, I've had a few*

*But then again, too few to mention*

*I did what I had to do*

*And saw it through without exemption*

*I planned each charted course*

*Each careful step along the byway*

*And more, much more than this*

*I did it my way*

*Yes, there were times, I'm sure you knew*

*When I bit off more than I could chew*

*But through it all, when there was doubt*

*I ate it up and spit it out*

*I faced it all and I stood tall*

*And did it my way*

*I've loved, I've laughed and cried*

*I've had my fill my share of losing*

*And now, as tears subside*

*I find it all so amusing*

*To think I did all that*

*And may I say - not in a shy way*

*Oh no, oh no, not me*

*I did it my way*

*For what is a man, what has he got*

*If not himself, then he has naught*

*To say the things he truly feels*

*And not the words of one who kneels*

*The record shows I took the blows*

*And did it my way."*

Can you relate to this song? Are you doing things your way that you feel stressed from month to month? Well I know I was stressed.

The individualistic mindset shows up in how we manage the money God has blessed us with. The world we live in is obsessed with stuff, instead of being content; we focus on wants and not needs. This self-obsession comes with a price. When I hit rock bottom financially there was so much chaos in my life. I felt helpless and there were many times my pride prevented me from seeking advice. Prior to my financial crises, I read all of Larry Burkett and Ron Blue's books on managing God's resources. Even though I received a BS degree in Finance and had a MBA degree, I still managed my money in a way that was not pleasing to God. I had to go back to what I learned about finances from God's word. I had to start all over again. Have you ever been in a situation that had to get worse before it got better? After my divorce, my financial situation definitely got worse, but over time it got better. I had to go through my life change so I could appreciate what God had blessed me with.

Chuck Bentley from Crown Financial Ministry says that there are nine financial symptoms that are associated with financial bondage that come about from this individualistic mindset:

1. **You think so much about money and the future that you have no peace with God and can't focus on things outside of day-to-day existence.**
2. **You can't give generously as you want to give.**
3. **You're not at peace living on what God has provided and often yearn for things you don't have.**
4. **You're not working as if the Lord was your employer. Perhaps you're underperforming, or on the opposite end of the spectrum and a workaholic.**
5. **You constantly argue with other family members over money.**

6. **You can't or don't pay off consumer debt obligations in full ea month.**

7. **You're considering a consolidation loan.**

8. **You're receiving notices of past due bills and charging items because you can't pay cash.**

9. **You're spending money as a form of emotional therapy.**

When you review the above can you say that these symptoms describe you? If yes, then you are in financial bondage. But don't worry! You can live a life of Faithful Finances Forever and I will share the Worldview vs. Biblical Worldview and provide steps to help you live faithfully in your finances.

# 3. Worldview - Consumerism

*In the house of the wise are stores of choice food and oil,*
*but a foolish man devours all he has.*

*Proverbs 21:20*

If you want to understand a person's view of money, view their checkbook because it will tell you a lot about their money management. Early in my life, if I had to show my checkbook to someone I would have been embarrassed because what I was portraying to the public was much different than what was in my checkbook.

Consumerism is an ideology that encourages the acquisition of goods and services in increasing amounts. The real definition is high consumption of goods and money. This ideology is selfish in nature and promotes materialism. There was a period of time in my life where my goal was to make a lot of money, get a big house, and drive several cars so that I can impress others, which I eventually achieved. I wanted them to think that I was a baller shot caller. Advertisers play an important part in this new mindset.

Businesses focus on appealing to wealthy customers because they know that they will make a profit. When we see the wealthy and the people we idolize drive cars, own huge homes we want to emulate them so we begin to spend money on the things they buy. Those that are not wealthy, middle class want to imitate the wealthy. I once saw Matthew McConaughey driving a Lincoln in a commercial and felt I had to go out and buy a Lincoln. But my purchase this time around would be based on a budget. I went to the table with a substantial down payment that made purchasing less stressful. My former car purchases were based more on emotion than the state of my financial situation.

Many times we purchase goods for the instant gratification because we believe the purchase somehow changes our status in life. This behavior is a reflection of the "microwave society" we live in and our desire to have things now. We are not willing to wait to accumulate wealth or plan our purchases. The 2008 economic recession is a perfect example of how people lost their homes or jobs without really having a savings to fall back on. This is the lifestyle society tells us to live and it violates God principles. The Bible has over 2300 verses that deal with the area of money. You would think that we would seek the Word of God to find the answers to our financial situations.

I remember my parents waited several years and saved their money so they could buy a house. Today, many families are buying homes and can't afford them. Growing up in New York our finances were based on one income. My dad worked while my mom stayed at home taking care of the children. With only one source of income they were still able to purchase a home because they saved.

Many people who live according to the gospel of Madison Avenue have the mentality of buy now and pay later. As we take on the consumerism of the world, we have a tendency to go into debt by using credit cards. William Humber says that – credit cards are a "means of buying what you think you need, with money you don't have, at prices you can't afford, to impress people you don't even know." Debt, according to Webster's dictionary is anything owed or an obligation. Debt is money owed to a person or obligation to pay another. They tell us that we should keep up with the Jones', therefore we take on the attitude of spending money we do not have. As we continue to follow the Madison Avenue (mindset) and go further into debt not realizing there is a cost to having debt. Not all debt is bad, but it does cost us our health through stress that leads to emotional, physical, and mental fatigue.

# Advertising Exposure

We are bombarded by advertisements on a daily basis. Many advertisers want you to focus on what you do not have so that you'll buy things you do not need. For example, a radio ad for a local car dealer says, "Get rid of the car you hate and buy the car that you love!" The car you currently have probably gets you from point A to point B, but maybe it's not perfect. This car dealer wants you to feel bad about the car you have now with the idea that if you spend money on a new one, you will feel better about yourself. We buy into what advertisers are selling and are going further and further into debt. Here are some advertising statistics:

- 1,500 -3000 Advertisements daily
- 1 million commercials before the age of 21
- $180 billion spent on advertising
- 7.5 hours/day spent on social media outlets

# Debt Statistics

- 76% of American are living from paycheck to paycheck

- 25% earn $100,000

- 46% have less than $800 in savings

- 22% have less than $100

- In 1970: 15% of Americans had credit cards; currently over 80% of Americans have credit cards.

Credit cards.com says that Americans have created billions of dollars worth of debt over the past 45 years and credit card debt has been the major cause. Total U.S outstanding consumer debt was $3.62 trillion as of May 2016. This figure includes car loans, student loans, and revolving debt. The total outstanding revolving debt which is primarily made up of credit card balances was $953.3 billion as of May 2016.

Nerdwallet.com did a credit card debt study in 2017 and found the following:

| Type of debt | Total owed by Average US households | Total debt owed by U.S. consumers |
|---|---|---|
| Credit Cards | $15,983 | $931 billion |
| Mortgages | $178,037 | $8.88 trillion |
| Auto Loan | $27,755 | $1.22 trillion |
| Student Loans | $47,047 | $1.38 trillion |

As you can see consumerism has a hold on the country, but if we are to begin lowering our debt we must first know how much we owe. Not only are individuals and our government are in debt, but so is the church. The church is made up of people and church leaders who are in debt that bring a debt mentality to the church. In Timothy Terrell's article "Debt and the Church," he addresses what should a church do when numerical growth overwhelms existing physical facilities. "If the growth is expected to continue, most churches would simply borrow the money from a bank and build the additional facility which is the most common approach. Some churches are able to pay off their debt with no problem; others will find their budget cramped for years until the debt is paid off. A few churches will be driven into bankruptcy and shame when unexpected events hinder repayment."

To get a real time understanding of how much the United States of America is in, visit http://www.usdebtclock.org

# 4. Is Money Your Religion

*People who want to get rich fall into temptation and a trap and into many foolish and harmful desires that plunge men into ruin and destruction.*

*1 Timothy 6:9*

Money has a way of luring you in like a hunter uses bait to lure an animal. The animal comes upon the trap thinking he has the food, but in the end the trap has the animal. There was a time in my life which I thought having a great amount of money would bring me satisfaction, but I found that over time it lead to destruction. Paul wrote in 1 Timothy 6:10, "It's the love of money that is the root of all sorts of evil." We must understand that money itself is not bad, therefore how we view money is the problem.

We see in this world people place money above everything including God and their families. The Prosperity Gospel would have for you to believe that if you are faithful you will be rich and if you are not rich, then you are spiritually weak. This is very toxic to the Kingdom. Wealth is not a good indicator of how faithful you are. There are also many people who present a doom and gloom perspective and it is a shame that many evangelical leaders use fear to get you to follow them. We must also be weary of who we get our information from. What we believe then shapes our view of the finances. As Christians our view should be Biblically based. We must remind ourselves that the God we serve is still on the throne and is in control even when we go through the financial storms of life.

We must put money in its perspective and realize that our self-worth is not based on money as so many people believe. We live in such a materialistic country and put our faith in what we own instead of the spiritual. People pursue money and end up depressed because they may not accumulate or inherit the amount of money they would like. There is a conflict in our economy and Christians should focus more on faith instead of fear. God's economy is one of love. When we are fearful, we will not look to help those that are in need because we want to hold on to what we think is ours. When we operate in faith everyone prospers because we seek what is best for others and not individual riches. Material wealth does not fill the void in our lives therefore we must seek God's kingdom first.

In his book, Virtue and Affluence, John C. Haughey touches on our insatiability for wanting more. He says,"A person may be wealthy, but the person's possessions do not guarantee life, security or happiness. The deception is this: If I have more of this or that which I desire, just a little more, then I will have life as a result of this more that I have." You probably heard other people say if I just had a little bit more money I would have no problems. In the Greek, Pleonexia means a passion for more. Pleonexia is the extreme and its means too much of a good thing. The one question I had to ask myself is this, "What is the purpose of the more that I now have?" The world we live in says that we should live to the extreme. This way of thinking is what causes us to go further into debt.

Later on in this book I ask you to list all the things you own. For just a moment think about your home, car, bank account, clothes, stocks. What did you determine? Is the stuff you own yours? We spend most of our lives acquiring stuff, but when we die we can't take it with us to the grave. As I got more into God's Word, I realized that the stuff I was acquiring was not mine and it did not define who I was in Christ. We are managers of God's resources and who I am has nothing to do with money, clothes, cars, my home, or savings. These things did not define who I was. God does not know me as the person with the nice home or car.

# 5. Symptoms of Excessive Debt

When I look back over my life, especially when I went through my financial crisis, I can truly say there were symptoms that I ignored because I was only focused on myself. I wanted to impress other people so that they would think that everything was okay. My motto was, "I want it all and I want it now." There was a book I read a couple of years ago called "Poser, Fakers and Wannabees," that helped me understand that I was a people pleaser. There are many people in this world that are trying to imitate the behavior, customs, or dress off someone they admire. I saw people at my job living in huge homes with several cars and I began to seek those things in my life. I looked good on the outside, but I was miserable on the inside. I was not making my payments on time, creditors were calling to make arrangements and I ignored their call. These were the symptoms that experienced when I was in excessive debt. Below are some other symptoms you may experience if you have excessive debt.

**Discontentment** - Hebrews 13:5

"*Keep your lives free from the love of money, and be content with what you have.*" I was not content with what I had so I began looking at the prosperity of others. Have you found yourself wanting what others have?

**Impatient** - Proverbs 21:5

"*The plans of the diligent leads to profit, as surely as haste leads to poverty.*" I was caught up in this microwave society and I wanted things now. I had my first home at 25 years of age and was not ready for the cost that came with the upkeep of the house.

## Misused Money - Matthew 6:24

*"No one can serve two masters. Either he will hate the one and love the other or he will be devoted to the one and despise the other. You cannot serve both God and Money."* Early on in my growth, I served only money because I did not know God. When I did give my life to Christ, I still followed the world's way and continued to strive for more money. I learned from the world that if you had money you were important.

## Greed - Proverbs 28:22

*"A stingy man is eager to get rich and is unaware that poverty awaits him."* With what we have we should bless and be a blessing to others that are less fortunate.

## Excessive Anxiety - Luke 12:29

*"And do not set your hearts on what you will eat or drink; do not worry about it."* When we are out of the will of God our anxiety over money increases.

# 6. Dangerous Consequences of Debt

The above symptoms were there every step of the way and my avoidance of these steps caused me to experience the following consequences of excessive debt. Have you experienced them?

**Enslaves the Borrower** - Proverb 22:7

*"The rich rule over the poor and the borrower is servant to the lender."*

In Roman times, the creditor ruled supreme and they had great power over the buyer. Not paying your debt was considered a crime. If you could not pay, the debt was transferred to your family and they had to work to pay the debt off. The person's estate was sold and if there was a balance left to the debtor and the family had to still pay the debt. I was so enslaved that I could not give to those in need in my family or church. Internally I felt bad when I could not participate. There I was driving a nice cars with a 5 bedroom home and I could not give. I knew I was not a good manager of my money and I could not give God a tithe. Do you feel like you are a servant to the lender?

**Enslaves Children** - 2 Kings 4:1-7

The biblical story of the widow's oil helped me understand that you must use what you have to get out of debt. This widow's husband was dead and the creditors came looking for payment. As I shared earlier, creditors looked to use children as slaves to pay back their dads debt. Servitude as a debt payment by labor was permitted in the Mosaic Law, but the bondage was limited. Can you imagine your children being enslaved for your debts? You are probably saying no, but we cripple our children when we do not teach them how to be stewards of what God has blessed us with.

### False Future Presumptions - James 4:13-15

I learned that when you borrow you presume upon the future. Many times we spend money now with the hopes that we pay our debt later. In a couple of years, we hope to have higher incomes. In this verse, James tells us we spend most of our time worrying about today or tomorrow, carrying on the affairs of our family or business making money, but we do not even know if we will be around tomorrow. Do you spend time worrying and focusing on tomorrow?

### Wickedness - Psalm 37:12

*"The wicked borrow and do not repay, but the righteous give generously."*
We participate in wickedness when we fail to pay our debts. When we are in debt we have a tendency to blame others for the debt and get upset when they ask for their money back. Have you ever got upset with a debt collector when they called you about making your payments? I know this all too well because I would get upset with them, but I was the one that signed on the dotted line for the loan or credit card. We made a promise to pay monthly payments over a period of time. I remember on many occasions I would stop answering their calls in the hopes that it will all go away.

# 7. Anxiety

Consequently debts brings about anxiety in our lives when we do not follow God's plan for handling His money. According to Webster Dictionary, anxiety is a painful apprehensive uneasiness of mind or fearful concern or interest, doubt concerning the reality and nature of the threat and self-doubt. The anxiety we feel is explained in 1 John 2:16. *"For everything in the world— the lust of the flesh, the lust of the eyes, and the pride of life—comes not from the Father, but from the world."* The eye is the lamp of the body and if the eyes are good, then your whole body will be full of light.

As I shared earlier, we view 1500-3000 advertisements daily and have viewed over 1 million commercials by the age of 21. What we see will determine how we handle our money. If we see the rich and famous driving nice cars, then we want to drive nice cars. We devote our lives by trying to keep up with the Jones', but we do not know how they achieved their wealth. With our eyes we feed our lusty appetites (gluttony, selfishness) and we think we deserve it. If we feed our eye with things of this world, then we will have anxiety and not peace.

As a kid growing up in New York City, my parents never taught me how to be a steward of God's money because they were never taught. When I got my first job after college I mismanaged my money. What I saw from other people was to spend and go into debt. I was single, with a company car, and was making good money. I was buying $400 suits and spending $300 dollars on shoes. I had 13 credit cards and each one had a balance. I was always looking for another job that paid more so I could keep up my life style.

In Daniel 3, Shadrach, Meshach, and Abednego did not bow down to the worldly ways and therefore did not have the anxiety we have when we bow down to money and status. The world said that they were to bow down and worship the King's image. King Nebuchadnezzar got upset with them and threw them into the fiery furnace. Keep in mind, when you begin to follow God's way, you will be ridiculed and talked about in a negative way. In the end, doing it God's way is very rewarding. As you read, take some time to examine your heart. What you are bowing down to? Once you do this, you will find the source of your anxiety.

# 8. Biblical Worldview

Now that we have had the opportunity to look at how the world views money and how it impacts our lives, let's take a look at the Biblical worldview of managing money. The Bible has over 2300 verses about finances and how to manage money, but most people do not go to God's Word. We are bombarded with over 1500-3000 advertisement daily, but we do not hear about managing our money from God's perspective in most churches. The Bible will help us to put money in its perspective and will help us realize that our self-worth is not based on money as so many people believe.

For the Christian, there is a conflict. We ask whether we should follow the world or follow God. The Christian must focus more on faith instead of fear. God's economy is one of love. When we are fearful, we will not look to help those that are in need because we want to hold on to what we think is ours. When we operate in faith, everyone prospers. We begin to seek what is best for others, not individual riches. We have already discovered that going into debt does not fill the void in our lives. Therefore, we must seek God's Kingdom first.

Why do many Christians struggle to trust God with their finances? We trust God with our lives when we go to work or fly on a plane. We ask God for direction with our jobs, relationships and children. But when it comes to our money, we think we know what is best. It was C.S Lewis who said, "Every faculty you have, your power of thinking or of moving your limbs from moment to moment, is given you by God. If you devoted every moment of your whole life exclusively to His service you could not give Him anything that was not in a sense his own already."

In order to really understand God's plan for our finances, we must first have a relationship with God through His son, Jesus Christ and we must be complacent in God. Complacency is when we have a secure satisfaction in God. When we have a secure foundation in God we will have joy as we go through the situations of life. This brings about a willingness to think about God's will instead of our own. We will begin to be transformed and we will begin to grow in God's likeness and our hearts will be changed. Our thoughts and how we spend money will begin to change, but in order for this to happen we must choose God's will over our own will. So the question we all must answer is who are we complacent in? What is it that you have a secure satisfaction in? Is it your status? Power? Money?

Once our wills are lined up with God's will it will be easier to understand the following concepts: God owns it all- Psalms 24:1 The psalmist says the earth is the Lord's, and everything in it. The world and all who live in it. When I went through my divorce, I hit rock bottom financially and I had to go back to the above verse to begin my financial recovery. I had a job, a car, and lived in an apartment with no furniture. It was as though I had to start over. I had to utilize the food pantry at my church for food because I could not make ends meet. When my children came over we could not watch television because I did not have one. This verse clearly tells us that the Lord is creator, sustainer of the entire world. He owns everything. This changes our perspective on money. If God owns it all then we are only Stewards of His resources.

A Steward is a manager of God's property. As a steward (manager) we will have a different perspective of the money we make. Every spending decision becomes a spiritual decision. We must go to God (owner) to find out how He wants us to spend it. The idea of ownership will express how we will handle everything God has given to us to control. I am reminded of Luke 16:1-2 (KJV), *"and he said unto his disciples, there was a certain rich man, which had a steward; and the same was accused unto him that he had wasted his goods. And he called him and said unto him, how is it that I hear this of thee? Give an account of the stewardship; for thou mayest be no longer steward."* In the Greek the word for steward is Oikonomia (oy-kon-om-ee-ah) which means administrator of a household or estate.

In this verse, there was a manager (steward) who handled the affairs of the owner, but wasted the owner's possessions. The manager knew he was going to lose his job so he began to plan for his future by discounting the debts owed to the owner and the owner was pleased. We will all have to give account for how we handle God's resources.

As you can see, a Steward has tremendous responsibility as they handle financial resources.  Just remember that God gives us all things to enjoy therefore, nothing belongs to us. God hold us responsible for how we handle these resources. In a nutshell, the owner has rights, but the steward has a responsibility to manage it correctly. In the past, for example, I had a riding lawn mower that my neighbor, on several occasions, asked if they could borrow it to cut their grass. If I allowed them to use it, I wanted them to be a good manager of the lawn mower because it belonged to me. My neighbor had the responsibility to care for it while they used it.

Since we are not the owners of our possession, only stewards, we are accountable to the owner. The owner has entrusted us with authority of our financial resources and we are not to do with it whatever we want, but manage it according to the owner's wishes. As you begin to change your mindset and transform your thinking on money, the following characteristics should begin to manifest in your life:

**Wisdom:** Psalm 24:1, *"The earth is the Lord's and everything in it, the world and all who live in it."* Realizing that God owns it all and he allows us to be Stewards (managers) of Gods resources. Debt-free people begin to handle money differently and seek to eliminate debt at all cost.

**Goal Driven:** Luke 14:28-30, *"Suppose one of you wants to build a tower. Will he not first sit down and estimate the cost to see if he has enough money to complete it? For if he lays the foundation and is not able to finish it, everyone who sees it will ridicule him, saying this fellow began to build and was not able* to finish." Debt-free people track their spending on a daily basis and utilize their budget combined with a periodic review of their financial plan to stay on course.

**Sacrifice:** Hebrews 13:16, *"And do not forget to do good and to share with others, for with such sacrifices God is pleased."* Debt-free individuals avoid luxurious expenses such as premium cable packages, excessive eating out, extravagant vacations, etc. They set a goal, make temporary budget cuts, and utilize a budget to meet their goals.

**Non-Materialistic:** Philippians 4:12, *"I know what it is to be in need, and I know what it is to have plenty. I have learned the secret of being content in any and every situation, whether well fed or hungry, whether living in plenty or in want."* The person who is determined to get out of debt realizes that money doesn't buy happiness and places less emphasis on "stuff."

**Patience:** Proverbs 14:29, *"A patient man has great understanding, but a quick-tempered man displays folly."* Debt-free people are not fazed by advertisements to make impulse purchases like the latest flat screen television, newest model cellular phone, or the hottest fashions/trends because they will not buy unless they can pay cash. They are willing to wait, work, and save for those items.

**Responsible:** 1 Timothy 5:8, *"if anyone does not provide for his relatives, and especially for his immediate family, he has denied the faith and is worse than an* *unbeliever."* A debt-free person puts the needs of their household first, lives on a budget, and gets out of debt. It is most important to see debt for what it is – financial bondage is a barrier for living the life God has for us. Having the ability to be patient, make sacrifices, and use wisdom in spending will help eliminate debt and eventually break the chains of financial bondage.

In a nutshell, these characteristics helps us to see the source (God). If we seek popularity, power, or pleasure, we will experience unfulfillment. But if we see God as our source, we get a glimpse of who God intends for us to be. Remember, it will take time to develop these characteristics. I know for sure you will fall short like me, but I am here to tell you that if you fail in the area of your finances just know that it's not fatal. It was very easy for me to get into debt and it took me 3-4 years to get out of my situation.

Hebrews 2:1 says, *"We must pay more careful attention, therefore, to what we have heard, so that we do not drift away."* I understood God's Word in the area of finance and I let myself drift away. The drifting did not happen instantly, but over a period of time. When I was spending money, I was not focused on God. I had to go back to what I heard and then anchor myself in God's Word again. God's Word has stood the test of time and I encourage you to anchor deep in His Word.

# 9. Guard Against Discontentment

In addition to changing your mindset about money and managing your money as God would have you to, you must guard against discontentment. Satan will get you to think on the past and how you had it easy. You will begin to question whether you should do it God's way. I had to deal with this when I was sitting in that apartment with no furniture or television. Has there ever been a situation in your life where there are things you're supposed to do, but you don't and things you are not supposed to do, but you do? You see there is a struggle that is going on inside us that creates tension, ambivalence, and confusion. We know within us that we should not be charging up debt that we cannot pay for, but we do it anyway. Paul explains this best in Romans 7:15, *"I do not understand what I do. For what I want to do I do not do, but what I hate I do. The struggle is real, therefore, we must guard against discontentment."*

I realized how prideful I was. It was easy to give the impression to others that things were going well because they never saw my checkbook. When it came time for me to reach out to my churches food pantry, I did not want others to know that I was struggling. Initially my pride prevented me from going inside the building because as a leader in the church I could not let people know that I was struggling. I was actually worshipping self instead of God. As I continued reading the Word I came across Luke 12:15, *"Then he said to them, "Watch out! Be on your guard against all kinds of greed; life does not consist in an abundance of possessions."*

You must also guard against envy. Envy is a resentful desire to have what others possess; wanting what they have to be taken from them. We are a country that is so envious of others. Are you envious?

In addition, greed is a force to be reckoned with. Greed is an excessive desire for wealth/possession. I know for sure that I am not the only one who had to deal with greed. We are greedy for approval, applause, status, best car, biggest house. John D. Rockefeller was asked, "How much is enough?" He responded by saying, "Just a little bit more." Do you love money? Then you will never have enough. The psalmist said the following in Ecclesiastes 5:10, *"whoever loves money never has enough; whoever loves wealth is never satisfied with their income. This too is meaningless"*

# 10. Sources of Discontentment

As we guard against pride, envy and greed, it helps to understand our source of discontentment. As individuals our source of discontent falls in to the following areas: carnal comparison, commercialism, and consumerism. If the truth be told, many Christians watch reality shows and begin to compare themselves with the individuals on the screen. These reality shows are not reality, but we look to get contentment from them. The increased use of social media allows us to access things we would have never had access to years ago.

As I have shared earlier advertisers know how to utilize media to make us feel less than we ought. We begin to compare ourselves with others. We must understand that the ultimate goal of commercialism is for the business to make a profit at our expense. They continue to show their advertisements over and over again with the hopes of getting us to spend the money we earn. They do not care if you go into debt. They want you to be controlled by stuff so they can get rich. So how do we relieve ourselves of discontentment? I must tell you that there is hope and a way out if you do not see a way out. If you failed in the past, failure does not have to be your future so keep in mind that failure is not the end. As you begin to analyze your needs and wants you must begin to ask yourself the following questions:

1. **What process/steps do i follow before making a purchase?**
2. **Do I expect a material purchase to resolve an internal issue?**

3. Are any of my purchase decisions based on what someone else may or may not have?

4. Are there any pains of my past that i am trying to compensate for in the present with "stuff"?

5. Are my desires for anything else greater than my desire to please God?

# 11. Practical Ways To Get Out Of Debt

Now that we understand the worldview and biblical worldview of managing money, you may be asking what are the practical ways to get out of debt. To begin the process you must first understand the money you have is not yours and that you are a manager of resources that God has blessed you with. To be a Steward (manager), you must do the following:

**1) Give A Tithe To God** - Since 1990, I have heard people debate over the issue of tithing. There are so many excuses not to tithe. One question that comes up is, "Do you tithe on the gross or the net?" Early in my Christian walk, I tithed on my net, but as I began reading God's Word I realized God owns everything therefore, I had to tithe on the gross. It all comes down to whether a person has faith enough to trust and obey the Word of God.

We must understand that the Bible is the official authority on all matters including our finances. I hope as you are reading this book, you are beginning to have a change in mindset. The tithe is the one area that is overlooked by many people especially Christians. I know so many people today believe that all their money and possessions all come from their efforts and not God. They refuse to give God the glory. It was God who allowed them to wake up every morning to go out and work. So, there is a financial dilemma in this world. I remember seeing a cartoon many years ago about baptism. The cartoon shows a pastor baptizing a candidate and the pastor says "when I baptize you everything that goes under belongs to God. In the last frame, we see the man's body under the water, but the man is holding his wallet above the water which is our financial dilemma.

Does God have control over your finances? We already established that God owns and controls it all. I learned that the tithe is an external sign of an internal commitment. Where you are with God will determine what you give back to Him. You can actually tithe your way out of debt. Matthew 6:33 says *"But seek first his kingdom and his righteousness and all these things will be given to you as well."* The tithe is God's way for the Christian. Malachi 3:10 says *"Bring the whole tithe into the storehouse, that there may be food in my house. Test me in this says the Lord Almighty, and see if I will not throw open the floodgates of heaven and pour out so much blessing that there will not be room enough to store it."* Presenting a tithe to God is not like going to Burger King. We can't have it our way. Essentially giving to God is an expression of our devotion to God. God gives us things to share and not just hold on to those things. True giving requires our head and our heart.

**2) Understand Why You Are In Debt.** I was always told, you must be truthful to yourself about yourself. In order to get out of debt, you must know how you got into debt the first place. I would also suggest that a husband and wife do this step together so that they will both have an understanding of their current financial situation. It is truly a blessing when a husband and wife work together in this area. The major reason for divorce is based around finance so when the two are on one accord with God as to how to handle money there will be less stress in the household. How many times have we heard about one spouse handling the finances and then something happens to that person, (death/ illness) and the surviving spouse has no idea of the household finances? I went into debt because my goal was to keep up with the Jones'.

**A) Gluttony - You never have enough or never full**

**B) Comparison - Keeping up with the Jones'**

**C) Accident - Health issues/loss of job**

**D) Ingratitude - Not being grateful for what you do have**

**E) Lack of knowledge - Many of us just don't know why and have no idea how to get out of debt**

**F) Bad habits**

**G) Impulse spending**

**H) Get rich mentality (schemes)**

Every person that is looking to get out of debt must also take inventory of what they own and how much they owe. If you put it down on paper, you will get a better understanding of your situation.  Use the tables on the following pages to list your possessions and creditors. As you take the time to do this excercise, I ask that you ask yourself the following questions to get a better understanding of how you first initiated your debts:

**1) How many offers of new credit do you receive monthly?**

**2) How many catalogues and email solicitations did you receive for the sake of consumption?**

**3) How many times have you paid late on your bills?**

# Posession List

List your possessions

(Item, Debt Balance, Need - Yes or No)

| Item | Debt Balance | Need (Y or N) |
|------|--------------|---------------|
|      |              |               |
|      |              |               |
|      |              |               |
|      |              |               |
|      |              |               |
|      |              |               |
|      |              |               |
|      |              |               |
|      |              |               |
|      |              |               |
|      |              |               |
|      |              |               |
|      |              |               |
|      |              |               |
|      |              |               |
|      |              |               |
|      |              |               |

# Debt List

List your debts

(Creditor, Outstanding Balance, Mininum Monthly Payments, Interest Rate)

| Creditor | Outstanding Balance | Min. Monthly Payment | Interest Rate |
|---|---|---|---|
| Visa | | | |
| Master Card | | | |
| Auto Loan | | | |
| Student Loan | | | |
| Mortgage | | | |
| | | | |
| | | | |
| | | | |
| | | | |
| | | | |
| | | | |
| | | | |
| | | | |
| | | | |
| | | | |
| | | | |
| | | | |
| | | | |

Right out of college, I applied for every credit card solicitation I received. Actually I had many of them while I was in college. I hate to say this, but I remember lying on the credit application about my income. When the creditor would call to verify income, the supervisor would lie about the income. They did this with all the students that were working part-time.

**3) Establish A Budget** - Luke 14:28-30 *"Suppose one of you want to build a tower. Will he not first sit down and estimate the cost to see if he has enough money to complete it? For if he lays the foundation and is not able to finish it everyone who sees it will ridicule him, saying, this fellow began to build and was not able to finish."*

67% of people do not have a written plan

76 % live paycheck to paycheck

Have you ever started a project and it took months or even years to complete? There is a neighbor that lives behind me who embarked on a project to add living space to his home last winter and the project has not been completed. The back of his house is an eye sore. It appears to me that he did not have all the money to complete the project.

A household budget is an itemized list of expected income and expenses that helps you plan for how your money will be spent or saved as well as track your actual spending habits. Though the word budget has taken on a more negative connotation over the years, invoking an image of pinching pennies or limited spending, a budget is really just a tool—and a great tool at that—to gain better and more accurate insight into your spending habits. If you do not have a budget can you determine why? To answer this question, you must be honest with yourself about yourself. Many people do not establish a budget because of the following:

1) **Fear: many people are afraid to face the reality of their spending behavior.**

2) **Lack of Exposure: Some people do not have access to financial resources**

3) **Myth: They think they are the only one without a written plan, it takes too much time, it's only for the wealthy**

After doing the budgeting exercise, if you find out that your expenses are more than your income, then you must to the following to get back on track:

1) **Cut back on spending**

2) **Increase your income (part time job) so you can pay down debt faster**

# Monthly Budget

| Items | Budget Amount | Actual Amount | Difference |
|---|---|---|---|
| | | | |
| Income | | | |
| Income Total | | | |
| Other Income | | | |
| | | | |
| Expenses | | | |
| Mortgage/Rent | | | |
| Household Maintenance | | | |
| Taxes | | | |
| Insurance | | | |
| Electricity | | | |
| Water | | | |
| Sewage | | | |
| Gas | | | |
| Phone/Cell Phone | | | |
| Trash | | | |
| Cable | | | |
| Groceries | | | |
| Entertainment | | | |
| Credit Card Debt | | | |
| Loans | | | |
| Child Care | | | |
| Fuel | | | |
| Car Payment | | | |
| Other | | | |
| | | | |
| Savings | | | |
| Retirement | | | |
| College | | | |
| Basic/Other | | | |
| | | | |
| TOTALS | | | |

TOTAL INCOME - TOTAL EXPENSES = $_____

# Spending List

| Item | Cost of Item | # of Items Purchased Monthly | Cost per Month | Cost per Year |
|---|---|---|---|---|
| Ex: Coffee | $1.75 | 10 | $17.50 | $210 |
| Dining Out | | | | |
| Take-Out | | | | |
| Premium Cable | | | | |
| Magazine Subcription | | | | |
| Show tickets | | | | |
| Cell Phone Bill | | | | |
| | | | | |
| | | | | |
| | | | | |
| | | | | |
| | | | | |
| | | | | |
| | | | | |
| | | | | |
| | | | | |
| | | | | |
| | | | | |

**4) Monitor Your Spending** - This is one area which most of us struggle. We struggle because we are not disciplined enough to keep track. When I saw what I was spending on a daily and weekly basis I was able to make adjustment. The one area I had to get a handle on was eating out. As you monitor you spending on a weekly basis, make sure you:

**1) Do not open any more credit**

**2) Cut up any credit card offers. You may want to opt out from any pre-screened credit card offers**

**5) Determine Your Needs Versus Wants** - Psalm 23:1 *"The Lord is my shepherd, I lack nothing."* We routinely confuse what needs and wants are. Webster's dictionary says:

**A) Need-to be needful or necessary. Required, be under necessity or obligation.**

**B) Want-To have a strong desire for something, to hunt or seeking order to apprehend, the quality.**

| Wants | Needs |
|---|---|
|  |  |
|  |  |
|  |  |
|  |  |
|  |  |
|  |  |

**6) Debt Snowball Method** - Proverb 6:6-8 *"Go to the ant, you sluggard; consider its ways and be wise! It has no commander, no overseer or ruler, yet it stores its provision in the summer and gather its food at harvest."* Debt, oftentimes correlated with water, is expressed by saying "I'm drowning in debt." On the other hand, debt has also been associated with snow as in having a "snowball effect." Debt snowball is an elimination strategy to reduce debt. To begin the debt snowball process, list all debt and create a spending plan. Using the debt snowball method, you would make the minimum payment on all your debt and when the smallest debt is paid in full, you roll the money you were paying on that debt into the next smallest balance. For example, if your smallest balance due is a medical bill, pay off that balance, take the money you were paying towards the medical bill and add it to minimum payment you were paying on the next smallest balance. Your snowball will grow larger as you tackle more debt. Keep in mind that it may take 24 months or so (depending on your situation), but you will see progress if you stick with the plan.

You may be asking why start with the smallest balance first instead of the bill with the higher interest rate/balances? Debt snowballers will begin to see progress quicker by paying the smaller bills first. By the time you work up to the larger bills, you will have more funds to apply towards higher balances." Becoming debt free not only relieves that "drowning" feeling, but allows you to establish an emergency savings or savings for retirement, investments, and other long-term goals. Remember God expects us to be good stewards (managers) of

His resources.

Here are some steps I had to follow to utilize the snowball method:

**1) List all your debts with balances from smallest to largest.**

**2) Review your spending journal and cut spending.**

**3) Review your cable bill, cell phone bill to find additional money. I have a friend who lowered her cable package and cell phone package and was able to save an additional $300 to put towards her other balances.**

**4) Use additional funds to pay off your debt, beginning with the smallest to largest.**

**5) After you pay off your first debt, take that payment, and apply it to the next debt-see the chart below.**

| Creditor | Outstanding Amount | Min. Monthly Payment | Debt Elimination Payment |
|---|---|---|---|
| Visa | $500 | $25 (20 Months) | Payoff #1 $100 + $25 = $125 (4 Months) |
| Mastercard | $1,000 | $50 (20 Months) | Payoff #2 $125 + $50 = $175 (5 Months) |
| Car Loan | $5,500 | $200 (27 Months) | Payoff #3 $175 + $200 = $375 (14 Months) |
| Additional $75 Found in Changing Your Cable Package | | | |

**7) Review Your Credit Report** - A credit report is a detailed report of an individual's credit history prepared by the 3 national credit bureaus (Experian, Transunion, and Equifax). The report is used by lenders to determine a loan applicant's credit worthiness.

**Important facts:**

- **Your credit report is not based on your income, race, religion, or cash in the bank**
- **Credit reports often have error therefore you can correct and dispute error without paying a credit repair company.**
- **By law each agency must respond to your dispute in writing within 30-60 days**
- **Credit accounts remain on your credit report for 7 years, bankruptcies remain for 10 years and credit inquiries 2 years.**

# Credit Report Major Factors

| Description | % of Score | Why Significant? |
|---|---|---|
| Payment History | 35 | Are you reliable? |
| Credit Utilization | 30 | Are your balances too high? |
| Length of Credit History | 15 | How long have you been using credit? |
| New Credit | 10 | Do you have too much new credit? |
| Types of Credit | 10 | Do you have a healthy mix (revolving, non-revolving, secured)? |

**Each year you can get a free copy of your credit report at annualcreditreport.com(every 12 months)**

As you can see from the chart, how well you pay your credit and your edit utilization make up the largest part of your credit score.

**8) Stay Away From Payday Lenders (Cash Advance) Or What We Call Predatory Lenders.** Predatory lending is the unfair, deceptive, or fraudulent practices of some lenders during the loan origination process. These lenders get the borrower to agree to terms that a normal borrower would take. Many of these borrower have lower credit scores (credit risk) and will agree to terms that are not appealing to get the loan. Predatory lenders take advantage by offering high interest rates. These include payday loans, finance company loans, rent to own, and zero interest offers. A payday loan is a type of short-term borrowing where a lender will extend high interest credit based on a borrower's income and credit profile. A payday loan's principal is typically a portion of a borrower's next paycheck. These loans charge high interest rates for short-term immediate credit. These loans are also called cash advance loans or check advance loans. Payday lenders charge borrowers extremely high levels of interest which can range up to 500% in annual percentage yield (APR).

For 18 years, I worked for a finance company that offered high interest rate loans to those borrowers who had low credit scores. These borrowers could not get a loan from a bank, so the finance company was the alternative. The loans that we offered were tied to some form of collateral like a home, car, furniture. I am ashamed to say that as someone who had the head knowledge about managing money I was susceptible to these lenders. During my divorce I took several advances. I took out the max every time. Since part of your pay went to the payday loan you had to take out more to pay your other creditors.

**9) Know Your Credit Score** - Luke 14:28 *"Suppose one of you wants to build a tower, will he not first sit down and estimate the cost to see if he has enough money to complete it?* The context of the above verse focuses on the cost of being a disciple. God wants us to understand that there is a cost to follow Jesus and we must consider what Jesus expects. To be a disciple the cost is that we surrender everything to him.

Like someone who builds a tower looks at the cost and what it takes to complete it. Poor credit has a cost when you take out a loan. You will pay more in interest if you have a low credit score. Your credit score is a small number with big impact. It is a numerical expression based on an analysis of a person's credit files. A great credit score can save you money by allowing you to qualify for the best terms and interest rates when applying for a loan for a home, small business, car, or whatever your need may be.

On the other hand, bad credit scores or no credit history has many downsides such as:

**1) Rejection for apartments, cell phone services, credit cards, and loans.**

**2) Higher insurance payments for cars and other property coverage.**

**3) Higher interest rates for any money you borrow which equates to thousands of extra dollars over a few years.**

Having a bad credit score makes many aspects of your life more difficult and expensive. Rebuilding your credit can take years. Many lenders choose to use credit scoring as a tool to help them predict if a borrower will repay what is owed and repay it on time. The score gives the lender an indication of a borrower's credit worthiness based on credit history data. Credit scores are based on credit report information typically gathered from Equifax, Transunion, or Experian, the three major credit bureaus. Credit scores range from 300-850; with the average credit score of about 675.

The charts on the following pages gives us a glimpse of the economic impact of our credit score. The lower your credit score, the higher the interest rate and the more interest you will pay over the life of the loan.

# Credit Score Impact - Mortgage Loan

| Credit Type | Fair | Good | Very Good | Excellent |
|---|---|---|---|---|
| Score Range | 660-679 | 680-699 | 700-759 | 760-850 |
| 30 Year Fixed Mortgage Interest Rate | 4.85% | 4.64% | 4.46% | 4.23% |
| Monthly P&I (200K Mortgage) | $1,056 | $1,030 | $1,009 | $983 |
| Total Accumulated Interest | $180,113 | $170,827 | $163,190 | $153,733 |

Source: MyFICO.com

# Credit Score Impact - Auto Loan

| Credit Type | Fair | Good | Very Good | Excellent |
|---|---|---|---|---|
| Score Range | 660-679 | 680-699 | 700-759 | 760-850 |
| 60 Month New Auto Loan Interest Rate | 10.71% | 7.86% | 5.68% | 4.32% |
| Monthly P&I (25K Mortgage) | $540 | $505 | $480 | $464 |
| Total Accumulated Interest | $7,403 | $5,316 | $3,782 | $2,846 |

Source: MyFICO.com

# 12. Conclusion

To achieve Faithful Finances Forever requires hard work. There must be a change in mindset from a worldview to a biblical worldview. Sooner or later, we must understand that the Bible is our authority in all matters, including our finances. Understanding the worldview that most people have today is very important. Understanding the worldview mindset helps us understand how advertising targets customers. It's important that you do not get caught up in the Gospel of Madison Avenue - an individualistic mindset in which we focus on self. Every financial decision is a spiritual decision, therefore, we must ask God to give direction. There are several credit boundaries that must be followed.

**1) Owe No One** - Romans 13:8 *"Let no debt remain outstanding, except the continuing debt to love one another, for whoever loves others has fulfilled the law,"* is clear that we are to owe love.

**2) Contentment** - Romans 12:2 *"Do not conform to the pattern of this world, but be transformed by the renewing of your mind. Then you will be able to test and approve what God's will is—his good, pleasing and perfect will."*

We must be content with ourselves and where we are financial. We cannot focus on others and how they are living. 3) Plan your spending- takes time and dedication. This is done through the budget which is a proactive written plan or guide. This plan helps monitor and maintain income and expenses. In a nutshell it helps direct where your money should go and will begin to help you stop spending more than you earn. If you follow the following steps, you will begin to move in the direction of Faithful Finances Forever.

**1) Acknowledge God as owner.**

**2) Admit that you need a spending plan.**

**3) Assess and track your spending.**

**4) Audit by reviewing the budget to see if you have a deficit or surplus.** If you have a deficit you must begin to cut back on spending. If you have a surplus begin to pay down any outstanding debt. Remember it's not how much you make, but what you do with what you make

**5) Credit cards are not cash.** - They should not be seen as an extension of income.

# 13. Appendix - Verses on Finance

## 1) God Is Provider

*1 Chronicles 29:14*

*But who am I, and who are my people, that we should be able to give as generously as this? Everything comes from you, and we have given you only what comes from your hand.*

*Romans 11:36*

*For from him and through him and for him are all things. To him be the glory forever! Amen.*

## 2) God Provides Material Blessings

*1 Timothy 6:17*

*Command those who are rich in this present world not to be arrogant nor to put their hope in wealth, which is so uncertain, but to put their hope in God, who richly provides us with everything for our enjoyment*

## 3) Barriers To Giving

**Selfishness** - *Proverbs 11:24*

*One person gives freely, yet gains even more; another withholds unduly, but comes to poverty*

**Don't Rob God** - *Malachi 3:8*

*"Will a mere mortal rob God? Yet you rob me." But you ask, 'How are we robbing you?' In tithes and offerings."*

**Don't Overcommitted** - *Luke 15:14*

*After he had spent everything, there was a severe famine in that whole country, and he began to be in need.*

**Have A Plan To Give First** - *Proverbs 3:9*

*Honor the Lord with your wealth, with the firstfruits of all your crops;*

**Indulging** - *Proverbs 23:21*

*For drunkards and gluttons become poor, and drowsiness clothes them in rags.*

**4) Guidelines For Giving**

**Regular Giving** - *1 Corinthians 16:2*

*On the first day of every week, each one of you should set aside a sum of money in keeping with your income, saving it up, so that when I come no collections will have to be made.*

**2 Corinthians 8:2-3**

*In the midst of a very severe trial, their overflowing joy and their extreme poverty welled up in rich generosity. For I testify that they gave as much as they were able, and even beyond their ability. Entirely on their own.*

## 5) Giving Rewards

*Philippians 4:19*

*And my God will meet all your needs according to the riches of his glory in Christ Jesus.*

*2 Corinthians 9:8* (Obedience is always blessed)

*And God is able to bless you abundantly, so that in all things at all times, having all that you need, you will abound in every good work.*

*2 Corinthians 9:6* (Generous givers are generously rewarded)

*Remember this: Whoever sows sparingly will also reap sparingly, and whoever sows generously will also reap generously.*

# Other verses on Money

**We Are Stewards** - *Genesis 39:4-6*

*Joseph found favor in his eyes and became his attendant. Potiphar put him in charge of his household, and he entrusted to his care everything he owned. From the time he put him in charge of his household and of all that he owned, the Lord blessed the household of the Egyptian because of Joseph. The blessing of the Lord was on everything Potiphar had, both in the house and in the field. So Potiphar left everything he had in Joseph's care; with Joseph in charge, he did not concern himself with anything except the food he ate.*

### We Should Not Be In Debt - *Proverbs 22:7*

*The rich rule over the poor, and the borrower is slave to the lender.*

### We Should Pay Our Debts - *Proverbs 3:27-28*

*Do not withhold good from those to whom it is due, when it is in your power to act. Do not say to your neighbor, "Come back tomorrow and I'll give it to you" when you already have it with you.*

### Do Not Cosign - *Proverbs 17:18*

*One who has no sense shakes hands in pledge and puts up security for a neighbor.*

### Pay Your Taxes - *Romans 13:5-7*

*Therefore, it is necessary to submit to the authorities, not only because of possible punishment but also as a matter of conscience. This is also why you pay taxes, for the authorities are God's servants, who give their full time to governing. Give to everyone what you owe them: If you owe taxes, pay taxes; if revenue, then revenue; if respect, then respect; if honor, then honor.*

### Jesus Approved Paying Taxes - *Matthew 22:17-21*

*Tell us then, what is your opinion? Is it right to pay the imperial tax to Caesar or not?" But Jesus, knowing their evil intent, said, "You hypocrites, why are you trying to trap me?Show me the coin used for paying the tax." They brought him a denarius,and he asked them, "Whose image is this? And whose inscription?"*

"Caesar's," they replied. Then he said to them, "So give back to Caesar what is Caesar's, and to God what is God's."

*Acts 2:41-47*

*Those who accepted his message were baptized and about three thousand were added to their number that day. They devoted themselves to the apostles teaching and to the fellowship, to the breaking of bread and to prayer. Everyone was filled with awe, and many wonders and miraculous signs were done by the apostles. All the believers were together and had everything in common. Selling their possessions and goods, they gave to anyone as he had need. Every day they continued to meet together in the temple courts. They broke bread in their homes and ate together with glad and sincere hearts, praising God and enjoying the favor of all the people and the Lord added to their numbers daily those who were being saved.*

*Proverbs 21:20*

*In the house of the wise are stores of choice food and oil, but a foolish man d evours all he has*

*Philippians 4:12-13*

*I know what it is to be in need, and I know what it is to have plenty. I have learned the secret of being content in any and every situation, whether well fed or hungry, whether living in plenty or in want. I can do all this through him who gives me strength.*

*1 Timothy 6:9*

*People who want to get rich fall into temptation and a trap and into many foolish
and harmful desires that plunge men into ruin and destruction*

**Giving Is A Priority** - *Leviticus 2:12*

*Bring the best of the first fruits of your soil to the house of the Lord your God.*

**Giving Is Done Promptly** - *Exodus 22:29*

*Do not hold back offerings from your granaries or your vats. "You must give me
the firstborn of your sons.*

**Giving Is Premeditated** - *2 Corinthians 9:7*

*Each of you should give what you have decided in your heart to give, not
reluctantly or under compulsion, for God loves a cheerful giver.*

**Giving Is Periodic** - *1 Corinthians 16:2*

*On the first day of every week, each one of you should set aside a sum of
money in keeping with your income, saving it up, so that when I come no
collections will have to be made.*

**Giving Is Personal** - *Exodus 34-20*

*Redeem the firstborn donkey with a lamb, but if you do not redeem it,
break its neck. Redeem all your firstborn sons."No one is to appear before
me empty-handed.*